If You Want To Be Treated Like A Queen "ACT LIKE ONE"

By Gregory L. Rosemond

"Kush"

If You Want to Be Treated Like A Queen "ACT LIKE ONE"

Copyright © 2009 Gregory L Rosemond "Kush"

Printed in the United States

Published by Kush El Publishing

Edited by Diya Nabawi, T'Sheria Ray, Zachary Ray and Sheri Williams

Library of Congress Control Number 2009901108

ISBN   978-0-578-01339-8

Sales inquiries should be forwarded to:

Kush El Publishing, LLC
117 Westwood Dr.
Simpsonville, SC 29680

E-mail: Kush_el@charter.net

www.kushelpublishing.com

If You Want to Be Treated Like A Queen "ACT LIKE ONE"

Table of Contents

If You Want to Be Treated Like A Queen "ACT LIKE ONE"

Introduction Poem

"Daddy's Little Girl"

So young and so fine, so innocent and so Devine

You've got your whole life ahead of you so open your eyes.

This street life and club scene ain't nothing but a thing. It's easy for you to be a failure but it is hard for you to remember that you are a Queen.

No longer Daddy's little girl, now you're Ghetto Child. You once had the world at your feet but now you're running buck wild.

It scares me to think that you've brought children into this world; do the sins of the mother soon get passed to her little girl?

Where do you draw the line?

You spend more money dressing up your body than you do expanding your mind.

Degrees in Micro-Club-ology, you can two-step but you can't even spell.

If You Want to Be Treated Like A Queen "ACT LIKE ONE"

You can drop it like it's hot but in the school of life you don't understand that you've failed!

When will you understand?

It's not about bouncing from club to club or man-to- man while selling your body for Nine Hundred and Ninety Nine Dollars less than a grand!

It's about expanding and advancing, elevating and proclamations. It's about building and living, upgrading and updating. It's about praising and raising your kids!

You make me want to call you out of your name but I know that's not going to change the way you compute things in your disillusioned little ghetto brain.

Deep inside you is the future while you are a make-up of our past.

You've got generations of strong black genes inside you to guide you.

You really need to listen to them and I hope that you truly understand that it is ignorant young disillusioned little girls like you that make it so hard for strong beautiful Black Women to advance!

Young sisters, it's time to free your minds!

If You Want to Be Treated Like A Queen "ACT LIKE ONE"

If You Want to Be Treated Like A Queen "ACT LIKE ONE"

PREFACE

The battle for our future survival as beautiful people of Nubian Descent begins here. We are nowhere, if we break the word down to its simplest form, it is two words put together now and here. So in other words we are nowhere which means we are now here and there is no time like the present to reeducate, re-involve, re-kindle and return our beautiful Women back to their original status,

Queen.

My sisters you have had to endure by far the most severe mistreatment of any gender or race of people on earth. You have watched as your men were drafted and shipped off to war, sold on the auction blocks, lynched and most of all turned out by drugs and left to die inside of an unjust penal system. If you want to be treated like a Queen,

If You Want to Be Treated Like A Queen "ACT LIKE ONE"

delves into the physical, mental and social make-up of how our young sisters' conscious levels need to be raised.

Our village has let our young sisters down by allowing our young men *(who are bent on chasing that paper)* to undermine the very fabric of our community. These young men are selling our young women's bodies in their music videos and calling our Queens "Bitches, and whores" not only are they selling their bodies but also their respect. This was made obvious by the comment that an Old washed up idiot like IMUS made about some of our beautiful Queens calling them "Nappy headed whores".

This book is a combination of my thoughts and my Spoken Word Poetry meant to spark the seed of revolution in the minds of all of my Queens both young and seasoned.

If You Want to Be Treated Like A Queen "ACT LIKE ONE"

Dedications

This book is dedicated to the Queen that gave birth to my incarnation on this earthly plain, My Mother Yvonne T Rosemond. To my sister, who guided and protected me until I became of age to take my place as her protector, Queen Stephanie D Rosemond. This book is dedicated to my Grandmothers who both now are residing in the ancestral realm Gaynell Thompson and Francis Louise Rosemond. This Book is to all of my aunts who have throughout my lifetime been an inspiration Deborah Goldsmith, Reshettia Thompson and Cathy Beauford. To the most important Queens in training better known as my young Princesses, Princess Stephanieka Rosemond, Princess Tayron Rosemond, Princess Tiniah Rosemond, Princess Kelia Rosemond and last but most definitely not least my lovely daughter, Princess Ayahani Amoor Rosemond. To my host of Queen Cousins, too many to be named individually but you all get the point!

If You Want to Be Treated Like A Queen "ACT LIKE ONE"

To all of my female friends who have kept keeping me grounded.

This book is my way of giving flowers to my 105 year Old Great-grandmother while she is still living MRS Annie Mae Rosemond! I love you all!

Poem # 1

"Never Forget Who You Are"

Never forget that you gave birth to the universe.

With your nurturing hands you have fed every kindred on the face of this earth.

Never forget who you are.

Never forget that you put the pieces of a shattered family back together, out of disparity you were able to produce life as you created man in your image after your likeness for you are the true Genesis of the BIBLE, my sweet generations of Isis.

Never forget who you are, always remember that you are a Queen!

Never forget that from your womb came creation! You gave birth to a lineage of Queens and Kings who led great Ancient Nubian Nations like

If You Want to Be Treated Like A Queen "ACT LIKE ONE"

Akhenaton, Nefertiti, Chaka Zulu, Cleopatra and Mansa-Munsa, The True Lion King.

Never forget who you are.

Never forget that you sacrificed yourself for your ancient Egyptian homeland and that you gave the most important element on Earth, yourself to the Romans not knowing that the Catholic Church under their commission would destroy your land in the name of antiquities and research.

Never forget who you are, always remember that you are a Queen

Never forget that your son Hannibal crossed the Mountains on elephant back and conquered Europe. He brought to the uncultured Europeans Art, Government, Science and Religion.

Never forget who you are

Never forget that you stood on the shores of West Africa and watched as the Colonial Terrorist stole your children and transported them to the

If You Want to Be Treated Like A Queen "ACT LIKE ONE"

Americas only to be traded under a new economic system called slavery. As you wept, you blew kisses of hurricanes to turn the slave ships around with your babies

Never forget who you are, always remember that you are a Queen.

Never forget how you told us to Swing Low Sweet Chariot, Hush Somebody's Calling My Name, and to Wade in the Water as you led us to Freedom through the Underground Rail Road passage.

Never forget who you are

Never forget that you sang songs of Southern Trees growing bloody leaves as they bore strange fruit with the blood of hanging Nubians dripping blood all over their roots.

Never forget who you are

Never forget that your mere presence commands respect and that only words like Sister, Mother, Queen or Princess are acceptable. Only words of

If You Want to Be Treated Like A Queen "ACT LIKE ONE"

Royalty are befitting to a Queen as complex and as beautiful as you are!

Never forget who you are

Never forget that you are constantly under attack not just because you are black but because you are Strong and Beautiful.

Never forget who you are

Never forget that the only way to kill the Colony is to kill the Queen and that our jobs as men are to protect you at all cost although at times you may think of us as the enemy.

Never forget who you are, ALWAYS REMEMBER THAT YOU ARE A QUEEN!

Chapter 1

"We need to be Brain washed"

Queens, we need to be brained washed! We need to wash our brains clean of all the European images of what is truly beautiful. We need to take away the self hatred bread into us by generations of oppression. We need to soak our brains in the waters of truth. We need to wash our brains clean of the way that we look at our homeland and her beautiful descendants who we will now be calling Nubians Residing in America.

I cannot in good faith sit here and blame European Americans for the plague of our young sisters not dawning their crowns. I am merely showing how self hatred has festered and has been allowed to continue to grow in our village (community).

Images of what is defined as beautiful constantly inundate the air waves through various mediums (*i.e. television, movies, commercials etc*).

If You Want to Be Treated Like A Queen "ACT LIKE ONE"

Something as simple as a baby doll has a way of creating self-hatred in our young Princesses (Queens in training). Please take a moment to answer these questions. Why does Barbie not wear Locs? Where is her afro? She does not have any Nubian features now does she? Why is it that all of Barbie's friends who have a darker hue of skin have straight European like hair? If you can answer these questions, then you are conscious enough to make a difference. It is your duty as a Nubian Queen to educate our young Princesses on how to stop perpetuating the cycle of self hate. We need to give them images of us (Nubians) to play with and find beautiful. In other words, create, support and buy black baby dolls!

Now my Queens please look into the mirror and tell me who it is that you see? Look at your body and tell me what it is that you see? As you look into the mirror, take a deep breath and gaze into your own eyes for 1 minute uninterrupted. Now, tell me who and what it is that you see. Do you see what I see? I see a strong, beautiful, giving, loving yet uninformed sister. Uninformed of who you really are.

I see a Queen!

Queens, American culture has declared war on you. This society understands that the only way to kill this Nubian Colony surviving in America is to kill the Nubian Queen. One method that is used to kill our Nubian Queens is to kill her image of herself. Make her believe that she is worth less than who she really is. In other words kill her self-worth. Once she has been devalued then images of her true beautiful self is replaced with images of what the American European sees as beautiful (*i.e. the Barbie Doll*). Cover Girl wants you to cover up your true beauty up girl! GOD did not make any mistakes when she made you. She made you "perfectly imperfect" to quote former Goodie Mob member Celo Green. Perfectly imperfect is the mindset that needs to be adopted by each of our beautiful Nubian Queens residing in America.

If You Want to Be Treated Like A Queen "ACT LIKE ONE"

There is nothing wrong with you wearing Locs, Afros, Braids, Perms, Low Haircuts, etc. Whatever you do, you make it fashionable. I personally am opposed to my sisters putting chemistry experiments on their hair to straighten it. Perms in my opinion makes you look more European and less natural. A side note, what in the world is good-hair? & what is bad-hair?

I am not knocking anyone who wears a perm; I only want to remove the age old stereotypical mindset of what is allegedly beautiful. If we examine the theory behind straightening our hair we will see that straightening combs and perms were another way of perpetuating a subtle form of self-hatred. We as Nubians residing in America have had to deal-with enough garbage than to have to continue to deal-with the issues that American Europeans have with our hair. Please listen to India Arie's song "I am not my Hair"

Images of what is or is not fashionable are currently being molded by the media, through advertisement campaigns. These advertisement campaigns are used by the make-up corporations and hair care companies to continue the subtle programming of self-hate amongst our Nubians residing in America. I understand that the perm allegedly makes your hair more manageable, however, the last time I felt my sister Stephanie and my first cousin Angela's Locs, they were both extremely soft and manageable!

My young and seasoned Queens, I need you to love your natural hair as part of the whole experience of loving yourself. Embrace the Nubian that resides within you. You are the Mother of nature. Everything about you is natural.

My Queens you must learn to trust your natural instincts by allowing your earthly maternal souls to guide you. My young Princesses you do not always have to live and learn. You should listen to our Seasoned Queens for they are the true veterans in this war that the American Culture has declared on you.

If You Want to Be Treated Like A Queen "ACT LIKE ONE"

This American culture is obsessed with food. As Americans we all like a little, and some of us a lot of seasoning on our foods. Our Seasoned Queens are like a perfectly seasoned meal which explains why each day more and more American European men are seeking the love and warmth of our Nubian Queens. Take the time to study our history young Princesses. Ask our Seasoned Queens to explain the historical behavior of some of the American European males. He has from slavery times been attracted to you. He has loved your nurturing breast (*which were used to feed his children*), your shapely-hips, enduring legs and firm buttocks. He has loved you so much that he sold your children on the auction blocks, sold and traded off your men. He has slipped in and out of your slave quarters to freely and forcibly mate with you. Strom Thurmond who was a known political racist almost died trying to filibuster (block) the civil rights bill in the Senate during the 1960's. His legacy is a classic example of how the American European male has hated us as a people, while wanting to love you at the same time. This has always been Americas' love/hate desire for you. My sweet Princesses you should want the knowledge of a seasoned veteran to educate you on how to survive as you journey through this state of confusion we call America. Look to your Grandmothers, Mothers, Aunts and Cousins for guidance. If none of them are there to guide you then any female that you respect can beacon you through this madness. Pull from their good qualities and emulate them. If you have any of the above mentioned role models that you cannot find any good qualities in, then you really need to change your environment immediately. Get as far away from those individuals as you possibly can. Put yourself around people who are trying to build. Anyone who discourages you from doing something positive (i.e. *buying a house, going to college, starting your own business*) regardless of who they are get away from them as fast as you can. It takes longer to build than it does to destroy. Books of encouragement such as this one are important in that they serve a dual purpose. This book is meant to destroy what is not beneficial to you. This book is also meant to build you up in the image of the great, beautiful, vibrant, goal oriented, selfless, hardworking, (*both living and residing in the ancestral realm*) Seasoned Queens who came before you.

We really need to wash our brains clean of the mental assaults that various entities in this American society have placed on us as a people. The face of welfare has always been portrayed as us! The face of crime has always been portrayed as us! The face of illegal drugs has always been portrayed as us! The face of poverty is portrayed as us! Everything negative *(according to the entities that control the media which controls the people)* has to come out of Africa. The West Nile Virus, The African Killer Bee and the biggest lie of them all, AIDS.

My children the purpose of this brain washing is to help us to relook at every aspect of us as Nubians residing in America. We need a social reawakening so that we can become an intrical part of the dawning of the Crown of Survival on our Princesses. I shudder to think of what all the countless young beautiful Nubian Princesses residing in America will have to face in their lifetime. Through my words I hope that I can arm all of my young Princesses with the knowledge of self! The true knowledge of who they really are. Let me make one thing perfectly clear, **THIS IS NOT IN ANY WAY SHAPE OR FORM AN ATTACK ON EUROPEAN AMERICANS! THIS IS THE HISTORICAL TRUTH!**

Poem # 2

"Picture That"

To gaze into your eyes is to stare into the struggle of a strong beautiful ancient black sister.

Seeing the world through your pain has caused me to go through a state of metamorphosis, transformation, elevation or better yet a sincere change.

Knowing that you have filled the shoes of both Mother and Father you never give-up!

You may fall down, but still my sisters you get-up!

My dedicated sisters, my educated sisters, Bright and Beautiful Young Women of the Nile.

You can hide your pain behind your looks, but it's your eyes that never tells lies.

So I am poetically painting passionate portraits of profound women such as your-self.

Each brush stroke different yet it is the same.

If You Want to Be Treated Like A Queen "ACT LIKE ONE"

You are much more complex than the labels of shame that this society has been adding to your name.

Names like Welfare mother, Ghetto-Girl, Prostitute or Ladies of the Night.

I'm adding labels of fame to your name like, Activist, Educator, Creator strong beautiful ancient black sisters so ready willing and able to fight.

You're no longer waiting to exhale after inhaling all this bull that you've had to deal with.

You've seen your sons murdered in the streets. You've seen your men hung from trees and beat.

You've seen your daughters turned out by drugs and left all alone to die on these cold cruel streets.

You would rather struggle on your knees than to beg on your feet! So if your man can not understand just how blessed and beautiful you really are, tell him to picture that!

So you are absolutely right, I'm poetically painting passionate portraits of profound women such as your-self, not those collagen injected, silicone filled,

artificial behind, wanting your black man mean
while hating you at the same time.

I'm talking about you poetically inclined, spiritually
divine; taking one step at a time my sisters you all
are so fine.

So, if your man cannot understand just how truly
complex and beautiful you really are, please tell
him here is a snap shot of you.

Now Picture that!

Chapter 2

"My Body is my Temple"

If the age old cliché' is true that my body is my temple, then Queens why is it that not only you but us as a people continue to put unhealthy foods, mis-education and ill thoughts into our bodies?

My Queens you possess the gateway into this world! No man, woman or child breathing has entered into this world without first coming through you, the gateway! The gateway that I refer to is your womb. Any person walking this earth who did not get here through the gateway would be considered an Extra Terrestrial or an ET. Since conventional thinking does not give credence to the concept of Extra Terrestrials then that leaves us with one overwhelming point.

That point is that you as the Black woman/mother would in essence be considered the G.O.D.-Of - Creation *(Mother of Nature)*. Nine months inside of you makes you my earthly creator, my comforter, my source of life. For my diehard religious people I am not stating that your mother is GOD, however, there are some overwhelming indications in religious doctrine that supports this belief. Genesis = Genes of Isis or Generations of Isis. Islam = Isis Lamb or Children of Isis. Israel = Isis Ra El. Isis is the mother of Horus the original story of The Mother Mary and Jesus. This story was taken by modern Christian religious doctrine and the name Isis (Auset) changed to Mary and the name Horus (Heru) changed to the name Jesus. This was and always will be an Ancient Kemetic (Egyptian) story! Ra or Amen Ra is the Sun God in Egypt. Most religions at the end of their prayers say AMEN which means the hidden one or let it be so! Last but most definitely not least El the most ancient name of the creator that Christians call GOD. I know this is a lot to absorb but this will be discussed in another book at another time! My Queens you are as ancient and as beautiful as the earth is old. Your story predates anything that HIS-STORY (history) has written about you. The Egyptians were not the modern day Arabs and they definitely were not of European Descent as portrayed in the media anytime the ancient story of Egypt is presented! They were Nubians. In other words they were and are you! Please read and study Chiek Anta Diop of Senegal.

I say this to both my young and seasoned Queens, that you are royalty. You are special, you are love and most of all you are loved! This leads me to my next set of questions. Why do we spend $150 on an outfit at the mall only to turn around and spend $5 on a meal? Why do we spend more money putting on our head than we do putting in our head? Now let's take a moment to answer these questions. Question number one is answered quite simply. We try to cover up what is truly beautiful by dressing like a peacock with our chest poked out trying to attract the opposite sex. We spend $5 on a meal because we spent the rest of our money on the

If You Want to Be Treated Like A Queen "ACT LIKE ONE"

Peacock suit that will be out of style by the end of the season.

Don't get me wrong we are a jazzy race of people. My Queens, hands down you are the jazziest of them all. I highly encourage that we support our black owned and manufactured clothing lines. We need to remember that our body is our temple so we do not need to put unhealthy $5 meals into our temple. We need to return to eating fresh fruits and vegetables. We need to return to farming, like what our seasoned family-members used to do. You know a garden in the back yard, a pesticide free garden! We need to eat lean meats and return back to being a self sufficient village.

Queens if our village is our body then we have allowed it to become sick with a cancerous growth. This selfish parasitic growth is feeding on our village. The growth that I speak of is being glamorized through the music. What happened to uplifting music like the songs that were sung by Marvin Gaye, Sam Cook and Donnie Hathaway?

If You Want to Be Treated Like A Queen "ACT LIKE ONE"

Where did the music go? What happened to the music moving a culture, not the music being called a culture!

Hip Hop is not a culture! Hip Hop is a voice, an avenue *(just like the media)* to let the world know our feelings, our struggles and our concerns. Hip Hop becomes negative only when some young hip hop serpents' spit venomous lyrics defaming our community and most of all defaming you the Queen. We have our values turned backwards. We really need to shut off the television and get back to the basics.

Let me make this perfectly clear, Hip Hop is not the cancer that is attacking our village! It is certain Hip Hop artists who glorify the villainous side of life. It is the same pseudo elated ignorant individuals who are bent on making a fortune at any cost. That cost includes selling out our entire race! Sisters these venomous individuals have you in your natural beautiful form doing things in front of the camera that should only be done with your significant other in the privacy of your home. My young Queens you do not have to shake and show your body just for a man to see that you are so fine. You see we strong conscious brothers are attracted to your smile and your inner beauty! Your inner beauty is what I am trying to get you to see. Look, your body is your temple so keep your temple clean! Cleaning your temple begins on the inside in other words with self respect, self-pride, selflessness and self-awareness. Know that you are more than what and how the media portrays you. You are more than your clothes! You are much more than the car you drive or where you live! You are so much more than what meets the eye. You are strong, you are beautiful, you are loved but most of all you are a survivor!

Queens, your temple is beautiful. Your temple is so beautiful that it is being emulated and cloned for the sole purpose of attempting to make the European American women's temple (*who were not blessed to have their domicile (body) to look as vibrant and as healthy as yours*) to look just like yours! These women (*who were once thought to be the standard of beauty)* are now injecting Collagen and Botox into their lips and other areas of their body's in order to look just like you. These women are taking supplements and are working out in the Gym on the stair-stepper machine in an effort to make their booty look like what you were blessed with naturally. These Botox Barbies are doing everything they possibly can to look full figured. Skinny anorexic is out. Meanwhile, full figured thick lips, broad nose, shapely hips and a firm buttock is back in. In other words you are being returned to your rightful position as the true Queen!

My Queens your temples are being destroyed by science! During the early to mid-nineties Doctors were giving out free birth control shots called Deprovera. I witnessed first-hand as my beautiful sisters who were getting those shots started to lose their hair and gain enormous volumes of weight. Queens you were used as guinea pigs. Your bodies were part of an experiment under the auspice of free. By now my sisters you should know that there is nothing in this world for free. Are you aware of the fact that Deprovera is what is used to chemically castrate men? Your temple is being desecrated and you are doing absolutely nothing about it. You are leaving your life in the balance. This body is all you have to connect you to this earth. Your soul belongs to the stars while your temple was made to survive on earth. Until such time that your earthly time is over, you must as the earthly gateway protect your temple. To put it quite simply, do not allow the negative images of you that are being portrayed in the music, on television and most of all being played out in our village by unconscious people, influence you.

My Princesses do not allow these young men to talk you into allowing them to enter into your temple with any part of their body except for their mind. Love is mental, not physical! Whenever you feel that the time is right for you to share your temple with that special person, then you will need to have known that person's mental make-up to determine if he will be beneficial to you procreating and raising the next generation of our village. My

If You Want to Be Treated Like A Queen "ACT LIKE ONE"

Queens you have done it alone for far too long and my brothers really need to step up. This will be further discussed in the Next Book title IF YOU WANT TO BE TREATED LIKE A KING, "ACT LIKE ONE"!

Queens a book that warrants your immediate attention that really needs to be read is Queen Afua's books titled;

Sacred Woman: <u>A Guide to Healing the feminine Body, Mind and Spirit</u> , <u>Heal Thyself for Health and Longevity.</u>

Poem # 3

My Sweet SISTERS

My sisters with fine skin tones like mahogany.

Deep dark chocolate, my sisters some things are bothering me.

I'm so sick and tired of seeing and hearing you being called out of your name treated like a female dog this here must change!

Emulated imitated your skin is hated the world belongs to you simply because you made it!

Mother of the earth, sisters of ISIS you stood strong through all the crisis and evil devices.

You cannot make it through to see tomorrow unless you make it through the night.

Blessed with the knowledge and skills to fight,

My sisters your mistreatment really hurts. I have felt your pain since you gave birth to this earth.

Daughters of NINTI this world really envies your facial and physical characteristics because they are plenty.

If You Want to Be Treated Like A Queen "ACT LIKE ONE"

Revlon has revolutionized the make-up industry trying to make your counterparts look like you because they envy your full lips & wide hips, nurturing breast, firm buttocks thick legs now what's next?

Inject die capsules to make them turn black while projecting images of skinny anorexic women to make you feel fat.

My sisters your mistreatment really hurts.

I have felt your pain since you gave birth to this earth.

Chapter 3

"Decisions"

My sisters the decisions that you make today can stay with you for a lifetime. My Queens you need to make conscious, well educated and well researched decisions. A decision can also be called a choice. So as a Strong Nubian Male I make the choice *(like my ancestors who came long before me)* to preserve our heritage for our future generations. Every young Queen/Princess of pre-birth and birth giving age carries our future. So the decisions that you make with how you carry yourself, as well as, how you treat your temple will have a direct- bearing on the rest of our lives. I know that my sisters living in and raising children in less than desirable conditions believe that there is no way out, but my sisters I tell you that there is always a brighter day. I know that this sounds familiar because you can hear this same message being preached about life and salvation on any given Sunday. I am not here to fill your hearts with another sermon! I am here to rally you together as the nucleus of a movement of conscious well educated spiritually connected *(to the truth of who you really are)* sisters. The nucleus of any family is the Mother. One day my young sisters you will be a Mother, a Grandmother, an Activist, an Educator and most of all a Role Model for others to emulate. My sisters, before you can lead our village, you need to follow the teachings of our Seasoned Queens. "No amount of education can teach you what life has taught me" is what my Royal Queen told me the day I graduated from South Carolina State University. Those words have and will stick with me for a lifetime. My mother told me that in order to keep me grounded because she knew that as we travel through this journey called life we tend to use words to describe us. Words like, Mother, Father, College Graduate, Millionaire etc. Words are just that, they can never describe us. They are used to make differences in us. They group us with certain elements of this society. My Queen Mother was wise enough back then to know that people are people and that we all breathe and that one day we all will die. I told you of my experience my young sisters to let you know that I still learn from my Seasoned Queen. This is not to say that I do not learn from my Father, Brothers, Uncles, Grandfathers, Cousins, Sons etc. because I do. However this book is about you, my Queens. The decision that I made to focus on you my sisters is one of ancient caliber. My Queens you have been severely victimized by labels of shame as opposed to labels of fame. You are beautiful!

Princesses our legacy is one of greatness. Our story is one of endurance. Our lineage is one of acceptance. Our make-up is one of strength and our souls are full of love. We as a people make decisions every day. Good, bad or indifferent, we make decisions. Some of our decisions help to build our village, whereas, by the same token some of our decisions ultimately undermines our village. We make decisions to support products that do not give back to our community. We tend to want to patronize European American businesses and turn our backs on our Black Owned and Operated Businesses. Some of our villagers act as if Black Businesses will give them inferior services. These individuals are the decision makers who can benefit from a self realization of how we as a people have been mentally brainwashed by the WILLIE LYNCH SYNDOME.

My sisters govern all of your decisions with logic. Never make an emotional decision. Sleep on your options before you make any decision. Turn to your seasoned Queens for guidance; they can save you from making the same mistakes that they may have made.

Decisions can often lead us to crossroads in our lives. This is the time that we should ask for divine guidance. I am led to think of one of the most conscious sisters to ever embrace music and who many of us call the mother of the modern Neo-Soul movement, Queen Erika Bhadu. Erika sang a song which words goes something like this "ooh ah I'm trying to decide which way to go, I think I made wrong turn back there somewhere". I quote this divine sister to say that in this life it is fine to back track and find out where you may have gone wrong. The path to Nirvana is not always an easy path and we often make decisions that lead us to have to turn around and regain ourselves. Warning! Never let your pride/ego cost you. What that statement means is that you should never let your pride/ego stand in the way of you succeeding.

My Nation of Nubian sisters, we are standing on the edge of time, an issuance of a new level of Blackness. The time is now! We have come a mighty long way but yet we have not come far enough. We have helped to create this culture that permeates negativity into our community. That's right, our community. We own it. It is our responsibility to claim it back and to clean it up. Our decision to stand for what is right in our community should over shadow what is wrong with our community. We claim back our neighborhoods one house at a time. We reclaim one street at a time and last but not least one life at a time. Sisters our decisions have lead us to a startling reality that we as Nubians residing in America hate to admit. We have allowed materialistic illusions of wealth and success to over shadow our instinctive Nubian trait of being community oriented. So let us commit to community service in our community. Let's give back not necessarily in the form of money but in the form of time. Let's make the decision to utilize our God-given talents to build up our community.

Poem # 4

I shed a tear

For all of the mothers who have lost their beautiful children to these street wars.

I shed a tear

For the systematic destruction of a race of people who are older than the concept of time itself

I shed a tear

For all the people dying over wars the wreak of personal vendetta

I shed a tear

For all the brothers and sisters doing time for crimes that they did not commit

I shed a tear

For entertainers who glorify derogative terms to describe themselves like players and pimps

If You Want to Be Treated Like A Queen "ACT LIKE ONE"

I shed a tear

For the same ignorant pseudo hero's blinding the masses of the people by calling my beautiful Queens, bitches and whores

I shed a tear

For the systematic mis-education of a future black nation by utilizing treacherous teaching methods to implement self-hatred

I shed a tear

For all the black business owners who has had to close down their businesses due to insufficient funds

I shed a tear

For my sisters whose babies have been taken from their wombs because they could not afford to feed themselves' let alone another mouth

I shed a tear

For a black nation who has bought into this false American Dream of equality, freedom, and justice

I shed a tear

If You Want to Be Treated Like A Queen "ACT LIKE ONE"

For a nation not demanding reparation for mis-education, desegregation, gentrification and most of all for the African holocaust that gave birth to modern day Slavery

I shed a tear

Save the babies from hunger, Free the minds of our children with the right education,

Stand up and demand that our Athletes and Entertainers take a more active role in being accountable for the images that they portray to our youth.

Free those falsely accused reparations for all people of Nubian descent who have been culturally raped and mentally abused.

Stand-up and Shed no more Tears, for the time is now for us all to take action!

I shed no more tears because,

I'M ALL CRIED OUT!

Chapter 4

"Why are we at War?"

My sisters, Why are we at war? I am not talking about this senseless ego lead war that has caused nothing but death and destruction in Iraq. I am taking about the war between the Nubian male and the Nubian female. Why are we at war? Everything negative in our community is not a result of the Nubian male. There are numerous influences weighing down on our community. We are carrying the weight of underemployment, mis-education, self-hatred and unequal-economics. Our community legs are becoming weak at the joints from all the excess weight. We need to trim the fat and throw our weight in the right direction. Let's begin by declaring a cease fire. This war has to end because it is taking a toll on our community in the form of our children. The cease fire that I speak of is between you my sisters and my brothers. We do not need to have a corrupt court system to tell us what we need to do to take care of our children. We need to better educate ourselves on how to raise our children. We don't need to misrepresent ourselves to each other, telling lies about where we live and what material things we have. We need to have open and honest communications. We need to get back to old school courting. Courting is different from dating in that courting required approval from the family. People met each other's family and got approval.

This war needs to end immediately and with immediate withdrawal of troops. We need to throw down our weapons and pick up our conversations. Sisters please don't continue to put our brothers down for we have had to endure that behavior from the American Mainstream for far too long. Brothers we need to quit calling our sisters out of their names and treating them like property. We do not **OWN** anyone. This mentality is what caused us as a people to have to go through the Nubian Holocaust.

Once we have come to an agreement and a cease fire has been established, we can then move into the next phase which is called a peace treaty. I know that as with any process, any community and any race of people there are going to be some naysayers or bad apples. We cannot cater our treaty around those bad few who tend to overshadow all of the good people. We must first sit down behind closed doors and lay all of our differences out on the table. This means our likes and our dislikes. The truth is required in order for us to reach a treaty. We must do this for ourselves. That means no one outside of our race is allowed in our closed door meetings. We do not need to report in to the overseer and tell them what we are doing. This is a private matter that should be held in our churches, black owned businesses and in our homes. We need to outline what is acceptable in our communities, schools and homes. We need to exercise our voice. This time the movement has to remain our movement. That means no can kicking. Yes sir master ignorant brothers or sisters spreading our business into the mainstream American culture. This war has to end! We have fallen for the oldest form of assimilation, *The Divide and Conquer Technique*. A nation divided can never rise. Our community is divided and it really needs to rise.

We do not need the same old individuals speaking on our behalf misrepresenting what we need while at the same time living lavishly. This must come from within our community. No one can better moderate and or mediate the terms and conditions of our Peace treaty than those individuals who are in the midst of the battle. We need to pull our youth into these meetings and let them tell us what's going on. We need gang leaders, ministers, activist, poets, writers, employed and unemployed to weigh in. This is an ongoing peace treaty upgradeable and updatable. This is a living breathing agreement between us as Nubians residing in America. Once we have rebuilt our trust internally, then and only then can we re-emerge on the national scene and make our demands stick. Our money goes a long way and can make businesses and governmental municipalities fall to their knees. If we use our economics as one of our weapons in our arsenal we can make our voices heard. Strength is in numbers with us working as one cohesive unit. I know that haters will state that I am preaching or teaching separation when in fact I am laying out a plan, a format or better yet an out-line for our community redevelopment. We along with our European American counter parts flexed our muscles on November 04th 2008 when we as Americans, not African-Americans, not Caucasian-American, not Native-Americans, not Hispanic-Americans, not Asian-Americans but Americans voted our first president of color into office. I say president of color because President Barack Obama is one of our children, meaning a child of the entire World. I tell you my sisters we are returning to our righteous status.

We have shown that through unity, we can make historic things happen. This juncture or period of time that we will call wood shedding is needed in order for us to re-strengthen our community so that we can return to the world-stage as a healed, educated force to be reckoned with. My sister you have been at the forefront of every grass roots movement guiding, leading as well as supporting the movement. Malcolm X said it best when he stated that in order to reach the brothers you must first reach the sisters. My Queens you have been leaders even without knowing that you were leading.

Unequal economics is one of the leading reasons that the two sexes are at war. The Nubian male for so long has considered himself as with any male of any race to be the King of his castle, the bread winner or better yet the sole provider for his family. The television show "Good Times" is a classic example of how my brothers had been acculturated to believe that he has to be the sole provider for his family. James Evans in one episode told his wife Florida Evans and I quote "No wife of mine is going to be working. It is the man's responsibility to take care of his family". James in many regards was like the seasoned Nubian males that I and so many of my brothers and sisters have grown up with. A strong black male full of pride wanting to be that bread winner and sole provider of his family, but with strikes against him. One of the strikes that I speak of is a deep rooted fear by this society of Strong Intelligent Nubian males. James Evans was a Strong Intelligent Nubian Male who had to deal with unequal economics something that is not uncommon to the Nubian Colony residing in America. My sisters our brothers are still being discriminated against because of a deeply rooted fear of the power that the Nubian Male posses in his soul. His creativity is stolen every time he speaks. He has been and in many cases today is still being blocked from competing with his European American counter parts in business due to an unlevel playing field. My father always instilled into my brothers and myself, that we had to be bigger, stronger, faster, smarter and more cunning than our Caucasian counter parts. He told us that we had to have more education in order to compete with them and their less education. In other words, a College Degree for a Nubian male is equal to a High School Diploma for a Caucasian Male. This has been a fact of life for the Nubian Community residing in America. My father never factored in the most devastating piece of the equation, the fact that the Nubian Male would have to compete against the Nubian Female. Yes, I said the word, compete! There should not be a competition between the two sexes but a cooperation to move our families and community to the next level. My Queens, there is no I in the spelling of the word team. I understand that the point is unequal economics. The definition unequal meaning not equal is part of the history that the Nubian Colony surviving in America has had to deal with. This fact is underscored by the history of pay differences on jobs, red districting by banks and the justification of eminent domain and gentrification by local governmental municipalities. Local governments around the nation have stolen our communities in an effort to revitalize their downtown inner city areas. Simply put we cannot afford to remain living in our own communities unless we work together to declare our historically African American communities as such, HISTORIC COMMUNITIES! We are not at war!

The 1980's dramatization of Nubian Family Life "The Cosby Show" is a format that we should strive to achieve. Please notice that I stated a format which means a guide. This does not mean that it has to be 100% exactly as seen on television. What I take from the Television show is that Cliff and Claire had a co-operation. No one person was greater than the sum of the total. The two of them had set predetermined objectives of raising their children into socially conscious well rounded holistic adults. Despite their differences they were always able to communicate to each other their feelings, meaning their likes and dislikes. Communication is the key to making a family and community survive and thrive!

If You Want to Be Treated Like A Queen "ACT LIKE ONE"

Poem # 5

Mama

We shared a lifeline, we shared a love!

We shared a thought together, we shared a soul!

Before my lungs could breathe you took a breath for me!

Before my eyes could see you were the eyes that gave sight to me!

Before my heart could independently beat, you put my biorhythm into motion!

Nine months inside of you in essence makes you my creator my comforter, my source of life.

You're the one who was unselfish enough to sacrifice because at birth you came close to death so that I could have life!

You're my Queen, my essence, my source my everything

You are My MAMA!

If You Want to Be Treated Like A Queen "ACT LIKE ONE"

I have seen as the bravest of men get scared and call for their mama.

I have seen the strongest of men in the face of death scream tell my mama that I love her.

The only time a little kid will lay down everything and fight is when someone says your mama.

You are my Queen!

You're my Essence!

You're my Source!

You're my Everything!

You are MY MAMA!

Chapter 5

Beautiful **I**ntelligent **T**houghtful **C**aring **H**onest

The highlighted or bolded text in the heading of this chapter has been a treacherous word thrown around in our community for far too long. I have witnessed it being used and as embarrassing as it is I have used the word myself. I have learned through my lifetime of travels and studies, that in order to change the meaning of something negative, add something positive to it. Eventually the negative will be canceled out. Bitch is not a word used to describe my Queens, but the words that make up the acronym Beautiful, Intelligent, Thoughtful, Caring and Honest which are words that are appropriate to describe the Queen of Creation. Queen Latifah's early 90's song "UNITY" stated it best "Who you calling a Bitch". Queen Latifah *(as she is appropriately called)* is a glowing example of how our beautiful Queens throughout our darkest of times have been trying to heal us. Our Queens have nurtured us, comforted us, fed us, forgave us and most off all educated us! So why do we degrade her?

My people replace the word bitch with any one of the following words and you will immediately see the conversation go from negative to positive whether it be an argument or not . The words are and the conversation should go something like this:

1) **B**eautiful I know you _____.

2) **I**ntelligently we can_____.

3) **T**houghtful how can I _____?

4) **C**aring what would you _____?

5) **H**onestly I know you _____.

If You Want to Be Treated Like A Queen "ACT LIKE ONE"

A conversation is two sided which means that my sisters you will need to also alter your vocabulary in order to achieve the desired results. That means that no matter how upset you get, use positive words to express yourself and you will see an immediate change in the conversation.

Positive words are words that build, words that create, words that encourage and most of all words that radiate love. My sisters you hold within your own breathe words of life and of death. Life is what you carry inside your womb. Life is what you have in your bosom. Life is what you ultimately produce. Death is not a natural phenomenon for you although death is a natural part of life. You have the ability to make the decision to destroy through your very words starting with the way you communicate with your creation (your children). I know that sometimes your children can test your very last nerve. However it is just that a test, so pass it! Begin by relaxing first, calm down and think things through. Think of the immediate result desired as well as the long-term result intended. Then and only then do you choose your words and actions wisely. Children are a blessing and at times can be testy but they ultimately need to be molded in a positive way to channel their energy in order for them to become positive in their thoughts and actions. So when the pressures of life gets you stressed out, do not respond as the negative word BITCH but in the positive term Beautiful Intelligent Thoughtful Caring Honest. My sisters I need for you to be the change that you want to happen in others. Hold your heads to the stars and become one, a star!

Think of a warm place, a place where it is never cold. Think of a place where you are always accepted. Think of this warm and glowing place where you can be you, a place where you are not judged but most of all a place where you are prepared for walks through this maze called life. When you think of this place, my sisters and my brothers, think of your mother or someone whom has been a mother figure to you. She represents the warmth of life and of love. Warmth is not associated with the word BITCH; however warmth is associated with the acronym Beautiful Intelligent Thoughtful Caring Honest. I know that anytime I think of my mother I always think of the warmth and glow of the sun. My mother has been and will always be the center of my universe. She carried me, she shared her life line with me, she shared her love with me and most of all we shared her soul. Nine months inside of my mother has made her my earthly creator. Remember a "BITCH" cannot create! Only a Beautiful Intelligent Thoughtful Caring Honest woman crafts unmistakable creations of love.

Poem 6

"Back to Black"

We need to get back to Black!

Back to when we did not call each other niggers or bitches we called ourselves brothers and sisters.

We need to get back to Black!

Back to when we were separate but not equal marching, praying, protesting and standing together as a people

We need to get back to Black!

We need to get back to Black Pride and Black Peace, Black Soldiers and Black Thugs coming together to generate so much Black Love.

We need to get back to Black!

We need to make a Black contribution to find a Black Solution to all the rhetoric and hate in this Constitution.

We need to get back to Black!

If You Want to Be Treated Like A Queen "ACT LIKE ONE"

We need to get back to Black Rhythm and Black Soul, Black Communities and Black Stores.

We need to get back to Black!

We need to get back to Black Entertainment and Black Fun, Back to enjoying shows like, Good Times, That's My Mama, The Jefferson's and Sanford &Son.

We need to get back to Black!

We need to get back to Black Political Parties, Black Power, and Black Family Reunions with brothers and sister looking out for each other every day of the week and every minute of the hour.

We need to get back to Black!

We need to hold our heads up high and say it loud to the tunes of James Brown's I'm Black and I'm Proud.

We need to get back to Black!

We need to get back to Black Poetry, Black Hair, Black Dance, Black Music, Black Owned Businesses, Black Families, Black Communities and Black Caravans with Black Women and Black Men along with our Beautiful Black Children walking Hand in

If You Want to Be Treated Like A Queen "ACT LIKE ONE"

Hand I am so glad to see that we are finally getting back to black!

Chapter 6

"Financial Responsibility"

My Queens and Kings if you notice for the first time in this book I address you my Kings as well. I am addressing both heads of our village because we need to teach the next generation of our community, financial responsibility. We need to develop a mindset of Appreciative Value as oppose to the current mindset of irresponsible spending habits on depreciative items. We need to stress the fact that land equals money. Man can make all sorts of automobiles. He can build different style of homes, but the one thing that man cannot make is land. Most wars have been fought over land. This quest for land dates back further than the time of Nubian Holocaust. As a result of our mistreatment we were promised 40acres of LAND and a mule which has never been delivered. Tribes would at times go to war over land. Gangs would fight turf battles over land in which both outcomes led to the acquisition of land. I am not in any way advocating the act of violence to acquire land. I am a proponent of teaching our children the proper way to acquire land with no bloodshed. Family, our money goes a long way; however we have one major problem as Nubians residing in America. We recycle very little of the money that we earn, back into our community. My sisters in particular I speak to you because of your ability to influence change in our community. I ask that you use your influence to advocate to the next generation, trust. Our families need to adopt a concept of cooperative collaborative business dealings in short we need to work together. We really need to manufacture our own goods and stand behind the services that we provide. We need to buy black products and services in an effort to rebuild the financial side of our community. We need to teach the next generation about how to create and maintain wealth in our community. We begin by focusing on revitalizing our village through the acquisition of real estate.

If You Want to Be Treated Like A Queen "ACT LIKE ONE"

We need to build infrastructure such as stores and barber shops in our own community. In doing as much we will provide goods and services in and to our village. We can benefit from reading the following speech made by Booker T Washington on September 18th 1895. We need to read this speech to our villagers i.e. our families, neighbors, co-workers and church members. This speech needs to be read at Family Reunions, as part of our Black History Month Programs, Kwanzaa Celebrations and studied during Bible Studies. This speech should be read at Poetry Sets or any where we can bring up the discussion of returning wealth into our community. We need to have our youth study Booker T Washington's speech on Atlanta. We need to discuss the significance of his thinking as Nubians Residing in America over one hundred and thirteen years ago and how applicable it is today. Please read and discuss:

"Mr. President and Gentlemen of the Board of Directors and Citizens:

One-third of the population of the South is of the Negro race. No enterprise seeking the material, civil, or moral welfare of this section can disregard this element of our population and reach the highest success. I but convey to you, Mr. President and Directors, the sentiment of the masses of my race when I say that in no way have the value and manhood of the American Negro been more fittingly and generously recognized than by the managers of this magnificent Exposition at every stage of its progress. It is a recognition that will do more to cement the friendship of the two races than any occurrence since the dawn of our freedom.

Not only this, but the opportunity here afforded will awaken among us a new era of industrial progress. Ignorant and inexperienced, it is not strange that in the first years of our new life we began at the top instead of at the bottom; that a seat in Congress or the state legislature was more sought than real estate or industrial skill; that the political convention or stump speaking had more attractions than starting a dairy farm or truck garden.

If You Want to Be Treated Like A Queen "ACT LIKE ONE"

A ship lost at sea for many days suddenly sighted a friendly vessel. From the mast of the unfortunate vessel was seen a signal, "Water, water; we die of thirst!" The answer from the friendly vessel at once came back, "Cast down your bucket where you are." A second time the signal, "Water, water; send us water!" ran up from the distressed vessel, and was answered, "Cast down your bucket where you are." And a third and fourth signal for water was answered, "Cast down your bucket where you are." The captain of the distressed vessel, at last heeding the injunction, cast down his bucket, and it came up full of fresh, sparkling water from the mouth of the Amazon River. To those of my race who depend on bettering their condition in a foreign land or who underestimate the importance of cultivating friendly relations with the Southern white man, who is their next-door neighbor, I would say: "Cast down your bucket where you are"— cast it down in making friends in every manly way of the people of all races by whom we are surrounded.

Cast it down in agriculture, mechanics, in commerce, in domestic service, and in the professions. And in this connection it is well to bear in mind that whatever other sins the South may be called to bear, when it comes to business, pure and simple, it is in the South that the Negro is given a man's chance in the commercial world, and in nothing is this Exposition more eloquent than in emphasizing this chance. Our greatest danger is that in the great leap from slavery to freedom we may overlook the fact that the masses of us are to live by the productions of our hands, and fail to keep in mind that we shall prosper in proportion as we learn to dignify and glorify common labor, and put brains and skill into the common occupations of life; shall prosper in proportion as we learn to draw the line between the superficial and the substantial, the ornamental gewgaws of life and the useful. No race can prosper till it learns that there is as much dignity in tilling a field as in writing a poem. It is at the bottom of life we must begin, and not at the top. Nor should we permit our grievances to overshadow our opportunities.

To those of the white race who look to the incoming of those of foreign birth and strange tongue and habits for the prosperity of the South, were I permitted I would repeat what I say to my own race, "Cast down your bucket where you are." Cast it down among the eight millions of Negroes whose habits you know, whose fidelity and love you have tested in days when to have proved treacherous meant the ruin of your firesides. Cast down your bucket among these people who have, without strikes and labor wars, tilled your fields, cleared your forests, build your railroads and cities, and brought forth treasures from the bowels of the earth, and helped make possible this magnificent representation of the progress of the South. Casting down your bucket among my people, helping and encouraging them as you are doing on these grounds, and to education of head, hand, and heart, you will find that they will buy your surplus land, make blossom the waste places in your fields, and run your factories. While doing this, you can be sure in the future, as in the past, that you and your families will be surrounded by the most patient, faithful, law-abiding, and un-resentful people that the world has seen. As we have proved our loyalty to you in the past, in nursing your children, watching by the sick-bed of your mothers and fathers, and often following them with tear-dimmed eyes to their graves, so in the future, in our humble way, we shall stand by you with a devotion that no foreigner can approach, ready to lay down our lives, if need be, in defense of yours, interlacing our industrial, commercial, civil, and religious life with yours in a way that shall make the interests of both races one. In all things that are purely social we can be as separate as the fingers, yet one as the hand in all things essential to mutual progress.

There is no defense or security for any of us except in the highest intelligence and development of all. If anywhere there are efforts tending to curtail the fullest growth of the Negro, let these efforts be turned into stimulating, encouraging, and making him the most useful and intelligent citizen. Effort or means so invested will pay a thousand per cent interest. These efforts will be twice blessed—blessing him that gives and him that takes. There is no escape through law of man or God from the inevitable:

The laws of changeless justice bind Oppressor with oppressed;

And close as sin and suffering joined We march to fate abreast...

Nearly sixteen millions of hands will aid you in pulling the load upward, or they will pull against you the load downward. We shall constitute one-third and more of the ignorance and crime of the South, or one-third [of] its intelligence and progress; we shall contribute one-third to the business and industrial prosperity of the South, or we shall prove a veritable body of death, stagnating, depressing, and retarding every effort to advance the body politic.

Gentlemen of the Exposition, as we present to you our humble effort at an exhibition of our progress, you must not expect overmuch. Starting thirty years ago with ownership here and there in a few quilts and pumpkins and chickens (gathered from miscellaneous sources), remember the path that has led from these to the inventions and production of agricultural implements, buggies, steam-engines, newspapers, books, statuary, carving, paintings, the management of drug stores and banks, has not been trodden without contact with thorns and thistles. While we take pride in what we exhibit as a result of our independent efforts, we do not for a moment forget that our part in this exhibition would fall far short of your expectations but for the constant help that has come to our educational life, not only from the Southern states, but especially from Northern philanthropists, who have made their gifts a constant stream of blessing and encouragement.

If You Want to Be Treated Like A Queen "ACT LIKE ONE"

The wisest amongst my race understand that the agitation of questions of social equality is the extremist folly, and that progress in the enjoyment of all the privileges that will come to us must be the result of severe and constant struggle rather than of artificial forcing. No race that has anything to contribute to the markets of the world is long in any degree ostracized. It is important and right that all privileges of the law be ours, but it is vastly more important that we be prepared for the exercise of these privileges. The opportunity to earn a dollar in a factory just now is worth infinitely more than the opportunity to spend a dollar in an opera-house.

In conclusion, may I repeat that nothing in thirty years has given us more hope and encouragement, and drawn us so near to you of the white race, as this opportunity offered by the Exposition; and here bending, as it were, over the altar that represents the results of the struggles of your race and mine, both starting practically empty-handed three decades ago, I pledge that in your effort to work out the great and intricate problem which God has laid at the doors of the South, you shall have at all times the patient, sympathetic help of my race; only let this he constantly in mind, that, while from representations in these buildings of the product of field, of forest, of mine, of factory, letters, and art, much good will come, yet far above and beyond material benefits will be that higher good, that, let us pray God, will come, in a blotting out of sectional differences and racial animosities and suspicions, in a determination to administer absolute justice, in a willing obedience among all classes to the mandates of law. This, coupled with our material prosperity, will bring into our beloved South a new heaven and a new earth." [1]

My Queens and Kings remember the context and the time frame in which this speech was written. This sobering speech was delivered over one hundred and thirteen years ago. This period of time was only 30 years after the abolishment of slavery and roughly 73 years before the civil rights movement. Booker T Washington was not the only leader with visionary insight to financially moving our community. Please do not allow the conventional thinking of mainstream American pop culture to prevent our villagers from studying and applying the works of our great philosophers. Those philosophers include Booker T Washington, W.E.B. Dubois, Marcus Garvey, Noble Timothy Drew Ali, Malcolm X, Dr Martin Luther King and many others whom I did not mention. We do not need to worry about what America thinks about whom we study or the applications we use in the rebuilding of our community. Our philosophers deserve to be honored as revolutionary transformative visionary people of Legacy who gave us the infrastructure to return our Village back to a place of prominence.

Poem # 7

"My Rays of Light"

My people don't you fret cause this life is a lesson.

Be thankful for what you have please count your blessings.

There are many paths that lead to the same place so you choose the one that you feel is truly right.

No matter what path you choose you will always be my rays of Light.

Every day is a challenge so manage your time, keep your life in balance and leave the pettiness behind.

Never allow life's disappointed to consume you for youcan learn from your mistakes.

Take it all in stride and understand that there are many lies that you must overcome in order to reach the light of day.

If You Want to Be Treated Like A Queen "ACT LIKE ONE"

There are two sides to every story even Satan had something to tell, for if everything was truly pleasant then we all would live in heaven and there would be no need for hell.

You can learn knowledge from anyone at anytime so open your mind and let your thoughts be free.

Even a man who appears to be homeless can teach you one thing and that is how to survive on the streets.

Always judge a book by its content and never by its cover!

Brothers always give all women the same respect that you would give your mother!

Wise words written on paper can be filled with lies and full of deceit!

Always remain one with nature and allow your souls to remain free!

My people don't you fret cause this life is a lesson.

Be thankful for what you have please count your blessings.

There are many paths that lead to the same place so you choose the one that you feel is truly right.

If You Want to Be Treated Like A Queen "ACT LIKE ONE"

No matter what path you choose you will always be my rays

of Light.

Chapter 7

"Breaking the Cycle of Ignorance"

My Queens, have you ever gotten tired of watching the same old rerun in syndication on television over and over again? Has the radio play the same song so many times that you wanted to just turn it off? Sisters, we have the unfortunate reality of merely walking through our village and watching the same old rerun being played out in syndication from generation to generation amongst our villagers. The same old conversation has been replayed and relayed from Grandmother to Mother and finally from Mother to Daughter for so long that conversation has become so monotonous that it is a turn off. This rerun is called the Cycle of Ignorance. Ignorance is not a word that should always be associated with negativity. It is defined as the lack of knowledge or lack of education. A cycle is defined as an occurrence that reoccurs or something that is repeated. My Queens we need to break through this negative cycle of allowing our children to settle for less. We can no longer allow our Princesses to live up to anything less than their abilities. I know that most people state that someone should live up to their potential but in the world of science potential energy is energy that is not in motion. Kinetic energy is defined as energy that is in motion. Our abilities are kinetically in motion where as our potential is what we build on and work on putting into motion. We need to end the cycle of ignorance by kinetically putting this rerun into motion and rolling it out of our community. I am inclined to believe that each one of us has a responsibility to the redevelopment of our community. It is our duty to adopt families within our community and encourage them to raise the expectations that have been set around education, community responsibility and the overall health of the next generation of our villagers. We together can move our village to the next level. My people please listen to the 1980 hit

If You Want to Be Treated Like A Queen "ACT LIKE ONE"

song "Every Generation" by the world famous jazz artist Ronnie Laws.

I was the first of my parent's children to graduate from College. While a student attending South Carolina State University, I met individuals who were third and fourth generation of Degree seekers. Through conversation and interaction with my then peers, I found that their families would not accept anything less than a Bachelors Degree in fact I had the privilege of meeting individuals whose families would not accept anything less than a Doctorate. I found this to be an astonishing feat coming from a family where the expectation was to complete High School. I was then and am now privileged & honored to be a part of my family's effort to break our Cycle of Ignorance. Because of the efforts and strides that my family has made in the areas of education, the workforce and the military, we have been successful in raising the bar of what is acceptable in terms of higher education, community involvement and social responsibility. I have been blessed to have participated and been successful in all three of the areas that have raised the bar of acceptability in my family. My young Queens I am not knocking anyone who does attend and or Graduate from College. I only want you "BE ALL THAT YOU CAN BE" to quote my old Army motto.

My sisters this book has armed you with the knowledge to be the catalyst for change in our community. It will be an honor for you to be considered a bench mark for our village to set our minimum acceptable standard of achievement. My sisters you are the embodiment of a culmination of generations of prominence. You represent the soul of our nation. The Cycle of Ignorance can only be broken through you. You are truly loved.

Poem # 8
"LOVE"

I want a love that will last a life time. I want us to be able to reincarnate and return to earth 10 generations from now and still see us present in our bloodline!

I want a love that is considered to be the greatest love of all. I want a lover who hears my heart's yearning, feels my soul's desires but above all someone to answer my loving call for love.

I want a love that will transcend both space and time. I want to be so deep inside of her nervous system that I become an electrical impulse traveling up and down her spine!

I want to love her the same way that Osiris loves Isis! I want our love to be the most treasured gift in her life you know priceless.

I want a love that is so strong that the sun becomes envious of the moon, I want a love that so deep that Saturn will shake of its rings and align itself to kiss Titan one of Jupiter's moons!

I want a love that has no second thoughts & no secrets, no inhibitions, no doubts and no secrets!

I want to watch the sun rise and set in her eyes. I want to smell the sweet aroma of love every time she passes by!

I want to fulfill her dreams and make all her fantasies come true.

IF you are Ms RIGTH, Then I want to Love You!

Chapter 8

"Love yourself"

My Sisters, you must love yourself before you can truly love anyone else. My definition of love can be summed up with only one word "Bond". Love is a bond that is between two people, so in other words when someone says I Love you, they are really saying I Bond with you. Some Bonds are unconditional like the bond between that of a mother and a child, whereas other bonds are contingent. Contingent is defined as conditional. A contingent bond is like that puppy Love that each of us experienced as children. Back then ones love would be dependent on whether or not the other person loved you. This type of conditional Love is in part responsible for the increasing number of Nubian Women not getting married. The marriage rate in our village ultimately has a long term effect on our village's survival, as well as how our village operates. Unfortunately the unconditional bond of marriage in some sectors of our village is not respected. This is in part due to us, *(meaning the post civil rights movement babies)* relaxing our standards of acceptability. Who better to address this issue of unacceptable standards in our village than myself? I am an unmarried with three beautiful loving children out of wed-lock, devout father! I am a United States Army Veteran who is fed-up with how his village has degenerated. I am a strong educated once lost but now conscious brother. Too many times I have witnessed statements such as this being made to my young brothers and I quote, "Because you have her pregnant does not mean you need to marry her". The above mentioned statement is unacceptable in that it helps to illegitimatize our community. I am not trying to preach to anyone because I have contributed to this terrible injustice done to our village. I find it very necessary for me to address what I have done. I am not proud of it; as well I am not jockeying to get the father of the year award. I am only doing what a real man is supposed to do. I have been there for my children, socially, economically, spiritually and mentally as my parents were there for me. Believe me, my parents sat me down each time I procreated and explained to me the importance and significance of marriage in that they have been married for over forty one years. I say this to say to you my sisters, choose your mates wisely. Learn your partner from the head down and not from the feet up. If you learn your partner from the head down then you will learn their mental make-up before you take a chance on procreating with someone who will not be beneficial to you nor our village. Love yourself and your body more than you love someone else.

I was blessed to come to the realization of the injustices that I had committed to my family and my village the very first time I laid my eyes on my daughter. All of my past transgressions became apparent to me when I looked into her beautiful little eyes. Nervous and un-assured, I knew back then just as I know now exactly what I have to do. I have to make sure that my Princess loves herself. I have to arm her with the knowledge of whom she is and where she comes from. I have to ensure that she has self-respect and most of all that she is conscious! I am tasking all of my Queens and Kings to sit our daughters down in front of the mirror and ask them to tell us what about themselves that they do not like. Take what they say and show them just how beautiful they really are. Exploit their dislikes by accentuating their uniqueness. Show them how their differences make them even more beautiful. Make extra sure that our princesses love themselves (*Perfectly Imperfect*). This same self esteem building technique applies to our sons as well. My people my focus is on our daughters because a man is normally only going to treat a woman the way she allows him.

"If you want to be treated like a Queen my sisters then ultimately, "Act Like One"! Act is defined as a performance: anything done for fictitious purposes.

If You Want to Be Treated Like A Queen "ACT LIKE ONE"

My sisters now that you have reached this point in this book, I can proudly say that the act is over! The time is now for you to claim your lineage, declare your greatness, demonstrate your leadership abilities, show your strength and ultimately be a Queen! No one can love you more than you love yourself so take the time to pamper yourselves. Take the time to better our conditions by helping to clean up our community. Seize a moment in time to pull other sisters into consciousness and help with the process of reeducating and mentally healing our brothers.

Sisters we need you!

If You Want to Be Treated Like A Queen "ACT LIKE ONE"

Poem # 9

"Recesses of my Mind"

Escaping the savage brutality of a mind boggling reality leads me to a place where I can truly be free!

No need for alcohol or drugs, no outside substance can take me to that place that lives deep inside of me.

I escape to the recesses of my mind

In my mind I can be a Super-Hero or even travel to the stars. I can walk on water or just listen to my bio-rhythmic section beat at the pace of my heart.

I escape to the recesses of my mind

In my mind I can fly without ever leaving my seat. I can slide down the milky-way and land right back on my feet. I transform myself into an Eagle and soar as I fly I transform myself once more. I become a rain drop and wash the pain & suffering of my life away, I mentally illuminate my nights just like the sun's rays

I escape to the recesses of my mind!

Escaping the hustle and bustle of everyday stress I get away to a place where I am truly blessed, where honeysuckles smell so delightful and the sun always shines.

I escape to the recesses of my mind!

I find myself seductively enticed by the thoughts of mentally escaping this world full of strife.

I pop in an Isley Brothers' CD and teleport myself to a place so deep beyond the sea.

I turn off the lights and ignite my candles. I burn some incense and dispense my worries deep into the sky. I meditate to regulate the pressure of a pulsating blood drive. I close my eyes and thank the Universe for allowing me to survive. I escape to the recesses of my mind!

Chapter 9

Time Waits for No One

My young Princesses please do not spend your entire life wishing you were older only to achieve the age that you thought you wanted to be only to then wish you were younger. Time is a measurement created to mark the passing of eras. Every day when we enter into our jobs we make little comments like "I can't wait until this day is over". Enjoy every minute and every day of your life; do not wish your life away.

Lateness for some odd reason has been associated with the African American community also called (CPT) Colored People Time. America needs to understand that Nubians Residing in America have a different concept of time. We don't follow the minutes, the seconds or the hours of the day because now is Colored People Time. Now is the time for us to seize the moment. Now is the time for us to reclaim our culture. Now is the time for us to rebuild our families. Now is the time for us to rebuild our community and ultimately now is the time for us to take charge of our own destiny. We are in a state of emergency with the future of our community in the balance. We really need to emerge and see that our Queens and our Princesses are the most important keys to our future survival.

Only through communications can we open the dialogue of change. We need to continue the quest for what our President, Barak Obama used to rally the nation together, Change. This time unlike previous times we need to keep this movement ours! The time is now for us to make that change!

Sisters do not grow up before it is your time. Do you want a cake that is half baked? Would you like to listen to an unfinished song? What about driving a half fixed automobile? We do not want anything that is not fully operational. Please take the time to go into the woodshed (*Schools of Life*) and learn who you really are. Get prepared to come out and make the change. You have time on your side so this time let's make it work. Let's make the commitment to each other. Let's make a commitment to our families. Let's make a commitment to our community and ultimately let's make a commitment to our creator. Time waits for no one so let's start right now!

Poem # 10

"Chocolate Sunshine"

Us meeting now,

Meeting here is a combination of many lifetimes!

I've felt your essence whenever you mother came near me.

I've felt the way you moved inside your mother's womb whenever you would hear me.

You were sent right here, right now to carry on my lifeline.

You are so precious, so beautiful, you are my Chocolate

Sunshine!

Your beauty is as majestic as the banks that grace the Nile.

Your words flow as gracefully as the curves of your lips whenever I see you smile.

If You Want to Be Treated Like A Queen "ACT LIKE ONE"

Your soul is as powerful as the sun's rays of light. You've guided me through darkness; you have been my guiding light.

All that I am is because I am a part of you.

All that makes my undying devotion to life is you.

All that I have been and what I may become is because you are mine.

I am so proud to say that you are my Chocolate Sunshine!

I love you my sisters!

Conclusion

Together We Grow

Life is nothing with no one to share it with. Queens our Forrest cannot grow without all the different family trees coming together to keep our Forrest from disappearing. Each year trees are lost due to families not replenishing their own family tree. More and more of my beautiful sisters are focusing on their Corporate America Careers.

This focus is causing more of my beautiful Queens to not want to have children because they believe that children will stifle their careers. Queens please understand that there is nothing more beautiful than the procreation of life. A branch cannot grow without the tree being present to feed it. Birth control has more than claimed its share of our branches (children). This faulty judicial system has chopped down acres upon acres of our forest. Success in Corporate America coupled with the

If You Want to Be Treated Like A Queen "ACT LIKE ONE"

American European male's desire for you my Queens is now claiming a substantial portion of our Forrest.

We are here in America trying to grow as a forest; in saying that we need to start by replenishing our roots. We need to cultivate the land that we've planted our forest in. One of the ways that we can cultivate this land is through re-educating our people as to who we really are! We need to cultivate our land by cleaning up our village (community). We need to hold those individuals who are responsible for destroying our community accountable. We need to stand-up and tell our story. Queens with all that we need to do to replenish our forest; we must first begin with you.

I hope that this book has given you the inspiration to find a young Princess and to educate her as to who she really is. For any brothers who have read this book I hope that this has been an eye opening experience for you to see what we need to do as Nubian men to elevate, protect and most of all

If You Want to Be Treated Like A Queen "ACT LIKE ONE"

love and nurture our women. Any Hip Hop artist who wants to debate with me concerning how our Queens have been mistreated and misrepresented in the music and the music videos, to put it bluntly "Get at me"! I send out a challenge to all the Churches to hold conferences, seminars and self help sessions on how to return our sisters to their rightful place. I challenge our people as a whole to quit allowing our differences to separate us, but to allow our likeness to bring us together. WE ARE THE ORIGIONAL PEOPLE AND WE ARE NOWHERE (NOW HERE). WE ARE NOW HERE TO RAISE OUR COMMUNITY BACK TO ITS PLACE AMOUNGST THE STARS. To all my young and seasoned sisters struggling thinking that no one loves you remember that I do. IF YOU WANT TO BE TREATED LIKE A QUEEN THEN THE TIME IS NOW FOR YOU TO BE ONE!

KUSH THE UNSPOKEN SOUL HAS NOW SPOKEN!

Bibliography

Works Cited

1. Source: Louis R. Harlan, ed., *The Booker T. Washington Papers*, Vol. 3, (Urbana: University of Illinois Press, 1974), 583–587.

If You Want to Be Treated Like A Queen "ACT LIKE ONE"

Special Thanks

To my Father for helping to give me life and helping to make me into a man, thank you King Oscar L Rosemond. To my Grandfathers both of whom molded me mentally as my role models King Oscar Rosemond and Ancestor King Jonas Thompson. To my Uncles all who contributed to us surviving in America, Ancestor King John Thompson, Ancestor King James Thompson, King Thomas Rosemond, King Diya Nabawi, King Kenneth Rosemond, and King John Beauford. To my Brothers who stood by my side through it all, King Timothy Rosemond, King Kelvin Rosemond, King Darren Rosemond. To my host of cousins "We Are Family" To my Friends for Life King Zachary Ray, Ancestor King Anthony L Rosemond, Ancestor King Charles Oliver, and too many more to mention, "we ride or die together". To my Nephews, I hope that I may be beacon for you all to follow, Prince Tajee Rosemond, Prince Deshun Rosemond, Prince Javion Rosemond, Prince Tavion Rosemond, Prince Tobias Rosemond, Prince J.Q. Rosemond and little King Solomon Rosemond.

But most of all to my Sons from Your Daddy with Love! Prince Dominick D. Rosemond, Prince Quinton R. Rosemond and My son by Love not by Birth Prince Jaylin Adkins! All of you get Ready the next book is for you. **If you want to Be Treated Like a King "Act Like One"**

KUSH

Booking info
864-430-8407

Reminiscent of water flowing down-stream, so does the words of this spoken word artist named "KUSH". Born and raised in Greenville, South Carolina, Kush began his humble journey into the world of Music, Writing and Spoken Word Poetry.

Influenced by a family deeply rooted in music, he began to write his own songs and music as a young student in middle school. As a freshman and sophomore in high school Kush's musical abilities flourished as he took advance honors jazz band, a course typically given to High School Seniors. Upon Graduating from Southside High School in 1990, he took his talents and joined the United States Army. While stationed in Uijongbu, South Korea, he was exposed to a culture and belief system that was vastly different from the culture and belief system of Mainstream America. He began to ponder the true meaning of the existence of Life. Honing his musical abilities through the use of words, Kush began to paint beautiful elaborate pictures with words.

Kush A.K.A Gregory L. Rosemond during his 9-year tenure in service to his country fulfilled his lifelong dream of earning a Bachelors of Social Sciences Degree from South Carolina State University in 1997. He never lost sight of his passion for words and music as he released from his collection of rhymes and poems, an independent single titled "KOUNTRY GIRLZ" in 1999. As the single made its way up the Internet chart on MP3.com, "KOUNTRY GIRLZ" finally settled at the number 2 spot behind HIP Hop's legendary artist Q-Tip with his hit "Vibrant Thing". The spirit of truth would soon dominate his soul to the point that

Rapology would soon turn into a term that he has coined as "Spoken Wordology".

The words continued to flow like water and now after 25 years of writing and 3 volumes of poems later, Kush has arrived. Having worked under the tutelage of world-renowned vocal trainer and singer Robin Brown, (*who has trained world famous artist such as Usher, Toni Braxton, TLC and most recent R&B sensation Ciara and Bobby Valentino*) Kush has followed the path laid by his poetic fore-parents such as Langston Hughes, Nikki Giovanni, Kalil Gibrahm, Gill Scott Heron, The Last poets and Dr Maya Angelou. Kush promises to pick up the torch of Spoken Word Poetry & Authorship, and carry it well into the homes and hearts of a new generation of readers & listeners. Kush's Debut Spoke Word CD titled "Chocolate Sunshine" and his Debut Titled Book <u>"If you want to be treated Like A Queen "Act Like One"</u> promises to revolutionize the Book and Music industry the same way that Hip Hop has changed the world. Behold the Age-Of-KUSH!

For booking Women's conferences, Spoken Word Workshops and Lecture series,

Please call us at:
(864) 430-8407 or

If You Want to Be Treated Like A Queen "ACT LIKE ONE"

Write us at:
117 Westwood Dr.
Simpsonville, SC 29680

E-mail us at:

www.Kush_el@yahoo.com

Check me out on the World Wide Web at:

www.kushelpublishing.com

If You Want to Be Treated Like A Queen "ACT LIKE ONE"

111

If You Want to Be Treated Like A Queen "ACT LIKE ONE"

If You Want to Be Treated Like A Queen "ACT LIKE ONE"